Piggy March

VANIR KAMIRA

An incredible journey

First published in Great Britain in 2023
by Anthony Eyre, Mount Orleans Press
23 High Street, Cricklade sn6 6ap
https://anthonyeyre.com

Book design by Emily Secrett-Hill
Cover image by Peter Nixon

ISBN 9781912945467

A cip record for this book is available
from the British Library

Printed in Italy

To my gorgeous son Max who has learnt so much from Tilly's achievements. He now knows that great things can happen with hard work and belief.

FOREWORD
PIPPA FUNNELL

"She had grit, courage and a very big heart, which is why she was so brilliant"

MUCH IS MADE of top riders and their achievements over their eventing careers, such as the likes of Lucinda Green, Mark Todd, and Ginny Elliott, to name just a few. They would be the first to admit that their achievements were due to the partnerships they had with some outstanding horses, those partnerships responsible for many of their great successes such as Lucinda's Be Fair, Toddy's Charisma, and Ginny's Priceless. All exceptional horses.

Vanir Kamira—I am going to refer to her incredible career in the past tense, even though she is enjoying an easier life and still very much alive—Tilly Bean to her close friends, was one of those very rare but outstandingly brilliant horses. Piggy, of course, is extremely talented and has many accolades to her name; she has had some wonderful equine friends but, as so often is the case, it was the horse one would least expect that made her dreams come true of winning the two "big Bs", Badminton and Burghley.

I don't think Piggy would mind me saying that Tilly Bean didn't ooze class, didn't have the biggest jump or the flashiest trot, but what she did have was something very special: what was between her ears and deep inside her chest. She had grit, courage and a very big heart, which is why she was so brilliant. She knew exactly when the important occasions were and boy, was she tough and really prepared to dig deep. She shone out like a beacon at these iconic venues.

I can't tell you the amount of times that Piglet would say before her dressage, "Oh Pipsy, I'm worried about Tilly Bean, she feels so scratchy." And, yes, she often used to look it in the warm-up areas but, between Piggy working her magic and Tilly loving being on the stage, this little bay mare was able to lift herself in the atmosphere. She would grow a hand taller and her stride would be a foot longer and she would dance her way to one of, if not the top spot of the dressage leaderboard. There came a point whenever I heard, "Oh Pipsy, you don't understand, she really does feel awful," I would just think "Yeah yeah yeah…" as they both delivered yet another stunning test in the low 20s.

When it came to cross-country she absolutely excelled—so, so brave, she made the toughest of tracks look simple. She had an exceptional turn of foot and was always one of the quickest. Fair play to Piglet for allowing Tilly Bean to run and jump in a slightly downhill balance because that was how she was built, a little downhill and on her forehand, and that is how she liked to go. Piggy was, of course, able to do this due to the trust she had built up over the years.

Showjumping was probably her weakest phase, yet she jumped many very good rounds with the guidance of her jockey, and those good rounds were often when it mattered. But I am sure that if it wasn't for the odd rail, she would have won many more CCI5*s including Burghley 2019 where Pig and I battled it out for top spot.

The one thing that seems astonishing about this little superstar was that, with the unbelievable record she had, she was never given the chance to represent her country at a major championship. If I had been a selector, knowing Piglet and this wonderful mare, they would have certainly delivered the goods.

I spoke to Piglet several times earlier in the year as she was really pondering what was best for Tilly Bean. She wanted my opinion as to whether she should do another Badminton or not. The only advice I gave was to listen to her gut instinct and trust her judgement about the feeling she was getting from Tilly, whom she and her team knew so well. Absolutely Piglet is a true horsewoman and she made the correct call: between her and Tilly's owner Trevor Dickens, they decided not to do another three-day event.

Thank you, Vanir Kamira for your amazing career, winning more than 2,000 British Eventing points. You are a great example of an outstanding event horse. You remind us all of the importance of having a big heart and courage.

CONTENTS

CHAPTER ONE
THE BEGINNING

"Tilly was a well-made, good-looking filly, who grew like a mushroom"

THE STORY REALLY started in Aberdeenshire when Kate Jackson, Vanir Kamira's breeder, bred her dam. Fair Caledonian (Georgia) was a thoroughbred out of Kate's Fair Words, by Dixi, born in 1995, and Kate admits: "I was a little disappointed. She was tiny, fine-boned and a bit of a weed.

"She matured incredibly slowly but had super conformation so I showed her once or twice in hand. One kind Scottish horseman once told me, 'One day, that little horse will make you famous!'"

Georgia wasn't what the market was looking for at the time so Kate took her when she moved to Ireland, enduring a certain amount of derision from the Irish horsemen because of her size— several asked what on earth Kate had kept her for. The mare never grew beyond 15.1hh.

"I always tried to breed horses that would be desirable, valued, handsome, trainable and sound. That way I could hope they would be well cared for and well loved. At the very least, they should be able to do a job, and a good job at that," said Kate.

Although never backed Georgia was easy going, and produced several nice foals. Vanir Kamira was born in 2005, at Kilnacloy Stables in Monaghan.

"She was a well-made, good-looking filly, who grew like a mushroom. She was gorgeous, more like her grand-dam than her mother," remembers Kate. "Vanir was the prefix I used on all of my foals, while Kamira is a nod to her sire, Camiro De Haar Z, with a K for me, and ending with an A for feminine, instead of O. I called her Tilly and was delighted that the name stuck with her.

"Camiro youngsters could certainly be headstrong, and Tilly was no different. She didn't stand out as being particularly tricky, but then I didn't ask much of them as babies. Mine were all taught to lead and load, which is more than you can hope for with a lot of Irish youngsters—and I had a lot of terrors through my yard! Trevor Dickens has told me that Tilly was a horror to back; I'm rather glad I never attempted it with her mum.

"My lasting memory of Tilly is how pretty she was as a youngster....

Fair Words, Tilly's grandam, with Kate Jackson, who bred Tilly, her dam Fair Caledonian, and Fair Words

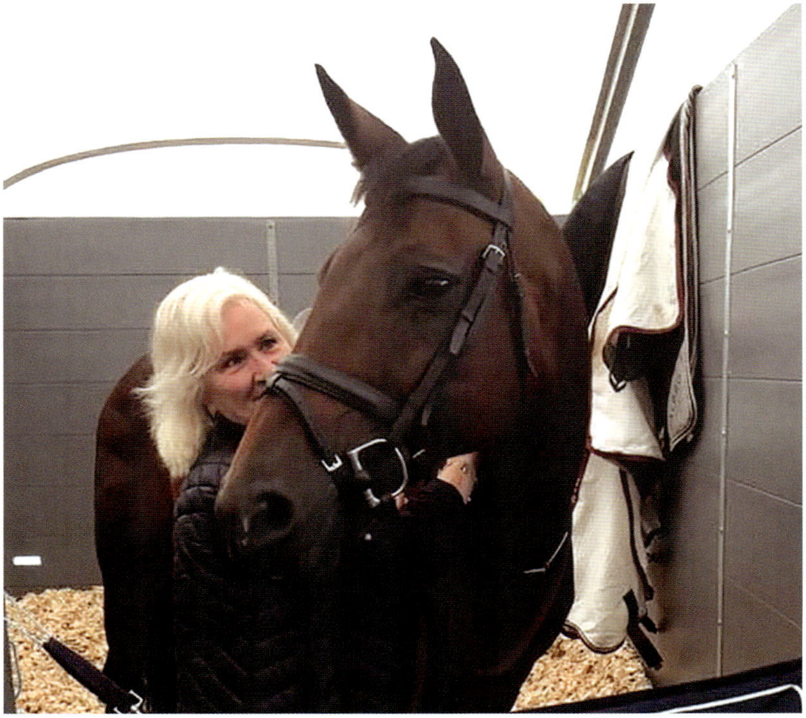

Above Left: Fair Caledonian as a yearling

Above Right: Fair Words with Fair Caledonian

Left: Tilly and her breeder Kate Jackson reunited

"Unfortunately, due to complicated leasing laws, I lost the tenancy on Kilnacloy and, unable to find other suitable premises I regrettably sold most of my stock. Tilly was sold to Trevor and Steph Dickens at Goresbridge for the princely sum of €4,000, if I recall correctly.

"I didn't see her again until she won Burghley in 2019, although I was in regular touch with Trevor who keeps me updated. Her well-being comes first and foremost with him; he adores the ground she walks on—which is wonderful for me, as her breeder."

CHANGE OF OWNERSHIP

"In 2007 we decided to get a three-year-old horse and produce it, hopefully to CCI5* level," explains Trevor Dickens. "We [Trevor and his wife Steph] were aware what was required as we had already taken a young horse from novice to

Piggy and Tilly with Trevor Dickens, his son Greg and daughter-in-law Sheryl, and Piggy's head girl Amy Phillips

He always believed she could do it: Trevor Dickens and Tilly after winning Badminton in 2019

the top level with our son, who was 20 when he did his first CCI5*.

"We agreed the horse would have to have loose movement, good conformation, a really good jump, an excellent temperament and, most of all, a brain. It also needed to have a good canter and walk, and be 75% 'blood' [thoroughbred]. We also agreed that the horse we buy must tick all of these boxes.

"Our first trip to Ireland took in Cavan. We saw probably 60 horses but nothing caught our eye. While we were there we got friendly with a man called Andrew who produced horses for the sales for Ronnie Hollinger, who had more than 100 horses at his stud—but there was nothing to suit.

"We came home and some months later went to Goresbridge Sales and saw some really nice young horses, but they didn't meet our tick list. So again, we came home and agreed to go one more time.

"The benefit of buying a three-year-old from Ireland is that you know that everything is for sale over there, and they haven't been wrecked. So off we went again to Ireland. We spent three days going around studs, and then went to Goresbridge.

"There were something like 100 three-year- olds there; nothing caught our eye apart from a horse in stable 147 who had a runny eye. Out of all those horses, we went back to her stable three or four times. It was showing on her breeding that the dam's side was unknown, so she was unsuitable. As fate would have it, toward the end of the day we got talking to Andrew who we had met at Cavan and said that we hadn't found anything.

"He said, 'Did you look at my youngster in box 147?' I said, 'The one with the runny eye?' He said, 'That's the one. She went through the sales but didn't make the reserve.' I said, 'I did look at her but she didn't have enough blood.' He replied, 'She has. She's full-thoroughbred on the mother's side and the father is Camiro De Haar Z. She is one of the nicest youngsters I have produced in years.'

"We agreed to meet him next morning at 8am, which was two hours before the sales started. She ticked all the boxes. Then we took her into the indoor school to give her a jump. Andrew put a jump up to the top of the wings; she picked up and soared over it with no effort at all. She did that again and we told Andrew to put her away as we had seen enough.

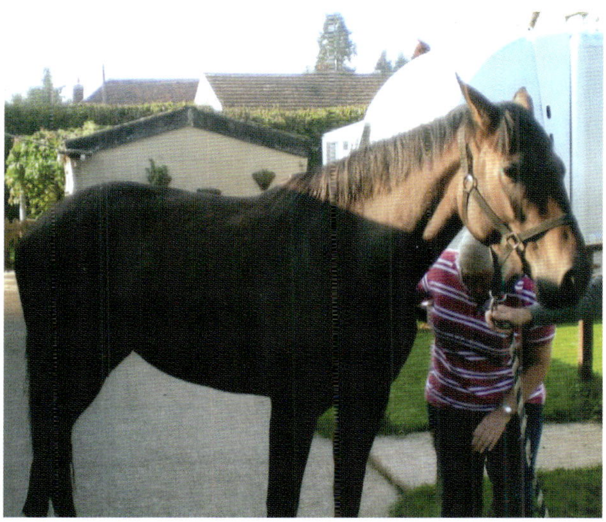

Tilly as a rather chunky-looking three-year-old

"I then spoke to Kate, the owner/breeder, and agreed a price. I remarked to Steph, 'This was meant to be and goodness only knows what she will achieve.'

"I sent her to be backed in the south of England. Apparently in 30 years they had never had a horse they couldn't back. But it wasn't going well—Tilly had thrown riders on the floor so many times. I asked if they would give it another couple of weeks and they said they would—fortunately. They broke her in and we brought her home."

TILLY'S EARLY EDUCATION

Showjumping producer Mandy Kent was an integral part in Tilly's early education. As Trevor Dickens says: "After being (reluctantly, on her part) backed, she was an absolute nightmare for six months, throwing riders off almost daily.

"I asked Mandy who, when she was younger, jumped for Britain, if she would showjump Tilly for 18 months to teach her manners. It was the making of her."

Mandy recalls: "I was sent her as a loose-jumping three-year-old. She was proving quite cocky, but I'd had horses for Trevor and Steph before so I took her on. She was quite difficult, always a bit gobby and challenging, but I adored her.

"She had loads of scope, loads of ability… I took her up to 1.20m.

"I get on well with mares and I understand that you ask, don't tell—but you can't let them get away with anything. She was always difficult in the mouth and always had an attitude but, basically, she was a gritter, which has come out in her future career. We got on well from start to finish, and it was gutting to see her go; I think she would have been a good showjumper if you could get her a bit more rideable."

Producer Mandy Kent showjumping a young Tilly

Trevor agrees: "Tilly was very headstrong and had many run-pasts, but she was unbelievably careful, and very brave. Mandy was the perfect person to teach Tilly discipline and manners. She was always destined to go eventing, but it was still hard for Mandy when I picked the mare up because it had taken her 18 months to tame the wild child."

For Mandy, she hadn't envisioned Tilly as a top-level eventer: "I never thought she'd go all the way. She's a little, gritty horse, a little terrier. She's not the prettiest, goes with her head a bit 'out', a bit free-range, not orthodox and round— but she always wanted to do it. It was her attitude of 'I want to be the best.'

"I've heard Piggy say, 'She's not easy, but when I climb on her she's with me all the way.' That is exactly what she was. She would always strive to get through the finish as best she could. I've followed her career the whole way and was so excited when she won Badminton and Burghley. And she has some foals, so the line will continue."

'She always wanted to do it," says Mandy Kent

Once Tilly was back with Trevor, the next step was to find the best event rider for her. "I had to find a rider who would be capable of eventing an opinionated mare. So I rang Yogi Breisner and asked his advice, and that's how she ended up with Piggy."

CHAPTER TWO

BECOMING AN EVENT HORSE

"She didn't give me an exciting feel—except from day one she was very brave and quick. She always found the flatwork quite difficult"

OVER TO PIGGY...

I FIND IT quite hard to remember Tilly at the start, to be honest. She came to me aged seven in 2012—I had a lot of horses to event; probably the most in terms of numbers of my career. It was the year of the London Olympics, so there was a lot of pressure. I had won the Olympic test event at Greenwich in 2011 and I was desperately hoping to be part of the British team there. As it happens, I had two horses selected—and they both went wrong, so I missed out. It was a difficult time.

Trevor and Steph Dickens were new owners to me and I just remember thinking that Tilly was a very weak young horse. She was a little mare, not strong in her body, and was going to take time to mature. She didn't cause me much grief, but at the same time she didn't give me an exciting feel—except from day

This picture of her was taken at Milton Keynes—she actually looks rather good here!

one she was very brave and quick. She always found the flatwork quite difficult and could only hold herself in a shape for so long, but you knew that would come with age and work.

Trevor and Steph used to take her home quite a lot, which has always been something I don't love as a rider and trainer; it's as important to know the horses on the quiet days as it is on the competition days.

As I say, I don't remember an awful lot about her that year, but in some ways that is how Tilly has always been—she just gets on with it, and comes out on top when you get to the critical moment where you need her to fight for something.

Looking back at her eventing record, it was fine—she started rather well by finishing on her dressage mark of 21 in her first BE90 at Solihull in April, and ended with three Novice runs in the autumn. She was always clear across country, and mostly showjumped clear, too.

To be totally honest I had too many horses, I was going through quite a lot of drama with horse injuries, the Olympics, various personal issues... I was also about to move yards which meant I needed to scale down on horses, and wanted to for my own head space.

Tilly was probably one of the first on the list to go; there were a lot of people in my life at the time that I needed to keep happy, and the Dickens' were new owners and therefore I didn't have that close relationship with them that comes with time.

I never for a second regretted letting her go; things happen for a reason at certain times, and I followed her progress the next season with Izzy Taylor with much admiration for them both.

Izzy cracked on and took her from novice to advanced in a season, as Izzy is known to do so well, with numerous wins and places at national level. Most memorably, they won the eight- and nine-year-old Advanced section at Aston-le-Walls. It was incredible to watch the progress they made and I was pleased to see it—fair play, Izzy—but I didn't for a second wish she was back with me; Izzy had the key for her at that stage.

A CHANGE OF JOCKEY AND CLIMBING UP THE LEVELS

At the end of 2012, Vanir Kamira moved to Izzy Taylor's Oxfordshire yard. Izzy evented her for a year and they whizzed up the levels from Novice to Advanced,

Izzy Taylor and Tilly winning the eight- and nine-year-old Advanced at Aston-le-Walls

winning an Intermediate, an Open Intermediate and an Advanced, ending the season with respectable results in the eight- and nine-year-old CCI4*-S class at Blenheim and the CCI3*-L at Osberton.

Izzy remembers: "Tilly was hot at that point, and she loved the cross-country. She was weak on the flat; she took years really to develop in that sphere—the best of her years were the last couple with you, Piggy.

"She could make up for her weakness with her jumping, and she's phenomenally fast. I don't think I ever, ever, pushed the rein forward, let alone kicked her. She did have a bit of a habit of leaving a leg on the odd cross-country fence, but she learnt from that. And she liked having her nose snuffling down towards the ground and that wasn't going to change. But that kept her up [on her legs]. That part of it wasn't the most pleasurable feeling, but the girls [mares] do try and stand up for you. The boys are, 'We're going down!'

"I don't remember much about her character, so she must have been straightforward. She was a very nice horse, not high-maintenance. She did get excited at events, but she had every right to do that. She loved the adrenaline. She won the young horse Advanced class at Aston-le-Walls on her first go at the level—and it was only her second season eventing, after all, which was very cool. She always fought for you, whether it was to stand up, or go between the flags. She was a fighter."

STEPPING UP TO FIVE-STAR

At the end of the 2013 eventing season, Trevor decided that he wanted Tilly to be in a yard that could accommodate more turn-out, which Izzy's set-up at the time didn't make easy. She was tried by a couple of other riders and she wasn't for them. Trevor asked me to have her back, and I thought he was mad to move her from Izzy. She was flying and, to be honest, I thought she was more suited to Izzy than me. I never regretted that decision as things happen for a reason, and so

'She always fought for you,' says Izzy Taylor, who evented Tilly for a year and took her up to Advanced level

many things are about timing and it wasn't the right time for me. Then Trevor rang the Australian rider Paul Tapner, who had won Badminton in 2010.

PAUL TAKES UP THE STORY...

"When Trevor and Steph Dickens called me, it was completely out of the blue. I'd never heard of them before, or of the horse they wanted me to ride. I was quite advanced in my career by then and had a wife, kids and mortgages to look after, so

I said, 'These are my fees.' That's normally the end of the conversation. But they didn't bat an eyelid. At that stage I didn't realise their horse already had experience with Piggy and Izzy, and that they knew how to deal with professional riders.

"They then told me the name of the horse— Vanir Kamira.

"I looked online and saw that she had been ridden by both Piggy and Izzy, and I thought to myself, 'OK, that means it's probably not a good horse, or they are difficult owners or something.' The mare had done a lot—Izzy and Piggy are

Riders like different ways of going and of doing things. Tilly feels on her forehand to me, and here Paul Tapner is clearly trying to get her to have more uplift in front, and he has showjumping boots on behind, which I didn't use. Her record with Paul was very good, so obviously both ways of doing things worked

not the sort of riders who would give up on a horse; they are both quality riders.

"My first impression of Tilly was pretty much the same as Piggy would say: 'Not much!' There's nothing wrong with her conformation or her attitude or her ability; she's just an ordinary horse. You don't get that 'wow' first impression. But Trevor and Steph had an undying belief in their horse. That's common among most owners—that's why they own them—but these guys were on another level in that respect.

"So I started riding the horse and she just kept getting better and better. Whatever I did with her, she just said 'Yes, I'll do it.' I very quickly started to realise that this was a serious horse.

"One of my key moments was when I rode her around Bramham in our second season together in 2015. I'd ridden another horse round earlier that morning and smashed myself up good and proper. Not something to be proud of—I shouldn't have been getting on the next horse— but I'd personally had some problems earlier in the season which meant Tilly was not qualified for CCI5* when she should already have been at that level. Bramham was my second attempt— my fault, not hers—so even though I wasn't really in a state to ride, I thought, 'If I don't, it will put the horse back another six months or another year,' so I felt I had to get her round.

"Bramham is a fairly tough old track. I could basically only use one arm and probably wasn't really with it, but I vaguely steered her round and she was clear inside the time without really trying. I was like, 'We have a proper CCI5* horse here: let's take her to Burghley.'

"Burghley was Tilly's first CCI5*. That was when Steph was seriously ill. It was a very tough time for the whole family, me included—by then I had become quite close to Steph and Trevor. They were a great couple, a very strong couple. Trevor would be the one to ring me but I could always hear Steph in the background—she was clearly sitting right beside him.

"I went out of the start box knowing that Steph was watching her 'baby' horse at Burghley, so I made the decision: you know what, it's all or nothing. I'm not going to ride this like it's her CCI5* debut and just get round for the experience.

"I knew she could do it, so I set off to try and make the time. I probably went out too fast, but with Steph in hospital I knew this was my only chance to let Steph see the horse was as good as she thought she was.

"Three-quarters of the way round the course Tilly got tired and we picked up 20 penalties. She'd had an amazing round until then. On the one hand it was obvious to Steph and Trevor that the horse coped brilliantly, with just a little whoopsie at the end when she was tired. On the other hand it was devastating for me, particularly when she jumped so well on the final day, but it was still nice to let Steph know that she had a proper CCI5* horse.

"You then fast-forward to the end of my riding career, when I decided to hang up my boots. I had many tough conversations with owners as I was handing in my notice to them, but speaking to Trevor—Steph had passed away by then—that was probably the only conversation that I really struggled with. I didn't really want to give up the ride on Tilly. I knew she was a proper five-star horse.

"Trevor's words to me were, 'I don't understand what you are doing,' and I was practically in tears at that point, thinking this was the only horse I really didn't want to give up.

"At Osberton that year, Piggy came up to me and said, 'Trevor wants me to take that horse back. I'm not sure I should. She couldn't really jump when she was with me.'

"I said, 'She couldn't really jump when she was first with me, and I don't think she could jump with Izzy either but, you know what, you take it round Burghley and the bloody thing can jump. She just wants to get to the other side, no matter how high the fence is. I would ride her round any CCI5* track. If you have been offered the ride back, take it. Piggy, take this horse.'

"I think she needed that confirmation that Tilly really was a proper CCI5* horse."

CHAPTER THREE

TOGETHER AGAIN

"I thought, 'It's not every day you get offered a five-star horse'"

TREVOR AND I had stayed in touch, and I had followed Tilly's career with interest. He had asked me at various times whether I would have her back, and I'd said no. I had enough horses, and she hadn't given me enough of an inspiring feel to want to try again.

She did her first CCI5* with Paul Tapner at Burghley in 2015, and at the same event the following year I was waiting to watch her run, but Paul had had a bad fall from his first horse and couldn't ride her. I sent Trevor a message saying that it was really sad and that I had been looking forward to seeing her go.

Shortly afterwards Paul announced his retirement from eventing, and Trevor rang me again. By then I had a very small number of horses— which suits me—and I thought, 'It's not every day you get offered a five-star horse,' so we chatted.

I said I would take Tilly in for the 2016 winter to try, but I didn't want to promise anything. Our son, Max, had been born in July; I was now a mum, and life was entering a different phase.

I remember seeing Paul at Osberton that autumn and talking to him about it, checking that he was definitely stopping—that I wasn't actually taking the ride off him—and that he thought Tilly was definitely a CCI5* horse. I'm not always the bravest and would be the first to admit that—I won't get on just anything with four legs and a tail and think that it's going to work out; it's got to be a feeling you get confidence from. Having Paul say to me: 'She IS a five-star horse' was enough for me to start with a blank canvas and a fresh set of eyes.

She had matured an awful lot, I knew she was brave, she wasn't spooky and if there was a fence in front of her, she was going to try to jump it. But the biggest thing for me was the belief that I got from Paul's words.

I was glad I had her for the winter.

When horses have been with other riders, they are used to their diets, their farriers, their systems—everything. It's something over the years I have become quite wary about. When I was young and hungry I was quite quick to try to change horses. I didn't really think injuries existed! Then you have a few problems—and I realised you have to give them time to make changes.

Tilly's a crabby little mare, who makes terrible faces at you and other horses in the stable. She wasn't carrying much condition when she came to us at our yard in Maidwell, Northamptonshire, and she was a grunty, groany, tail-swishy, highly-strung mare who was a bad traveller and a bad eater. She goes from stuffy to a bit mad and crazy just like that, and I wanted her to relax.

We started the whole process of trying to make her feel more comfortable. She had ulcers and was treated for them; I put her on the hormone treatment Regumate, which definitely helped, and I spent a lot of time with her.

Particularly in the early stages of her "second career" with me, Tilly wasn't a good eater and would go off her food very quickly. And when you travelled her anywhere, the weight you'd started to get on her would disappear immediately. We tried her with lots of different feeds without really getting anywhere until a good friend, Mitch Doyle, who had had loads of experience in the racing world, came to the yard to try to help me. I remember Mitch saying two things. The first

Winter 2016. The pictures here illustrate how I found Tilly to ride in the first few months that she came back to me. She was high on adrenaline and would get very hot quickly and break out in sweat easily (right-hand page). She looks much 'sportier' and lighter than she did later in her career. I worked hard on getting her to relax and to be calmer. Until she did that, I couldn't get more weight and muscle on her. The jumping picture shows the quick, tight, hurdley-type feel that gave me over a fence

was that Tilly had fantastic limbs and was a horse who was really worth bothering with and putting time into.

The second, when I explained that I very much wanted to get more muscle and condition on her but I was struggling to get her to eat, was that I should put a bucket of nuts outside her stable with a small cup in it. She was to be given half a cup of nuts at a time, in a bowl on the floor of her stable. If after 10 minutes she hadn't eaten it, I was to take it away. Every time I passed Tilly's stable, I was to try again—but never with more than half a cup of nuts. It was psychological; if a person with an eating disorder was given a plate piled with food, they wouldn't be able to face it. But if you gave them a plate with a very small amount on it, they might feel capable of tackling it, slowly.

This method taught Tilly to eat. In time, and over a period of 24 hours, she would eat the whole of her bucket of feed. What she had eaten through Mitch's system of drip-feeding during the day, she'd finish at night. Every time we went into her stable and put her headcollar on, or was tacked up or untacked, she'd have her little cup of nuts, so it felt more like treats to her than a meal.

It was quite a slow process, and right to the end of her career she was running round those huge Badminton and Burghley tracks on Hi Fibre nuts! No supplements, apart from the muscle relaxer Nupafeed, which we syringed into her a few times a day before she went cross-country at her last few CCI5* events. It contains magnesium and is obviously allowed under FEI rules, and definitely made a difference to her tying-up issue.

Her propensity to tie-up [when a horse's muscles go into spasm and cramp, which can cause muscle damage] meant we never ventured into the normal high-energy, high-protein feeds that the vast majority of competition horses are given.

Eventually Tilly transformed in size—muscle and condition—and we ended up having to diet her before her major events in the latter years because she actually became quite porky, which I never would have believed possible.

The travelling was something else we had to sort out. She had been in an accident before she came back to me, and used to get very upset. During that winter of 2016/2017, I took her to lots of very low-key dressage shows, just me and her, going slowly in the lorry with lots and lots of space to help her get over her fear of travelling. At first I took out all of the partitions and put her in loose, to see where she wanted to position herself, because in a wagon with partitions she kept trying to go down every time you applied the brakes, no matter how quietly you did it.

Thankfully I didn't have a great many horses at that point—I spent most of my time taking Tilly on long, slow, very boring days out and drip-feeding her dry nuts!

In the end she travelled as a normal horse, but we always only ever took a maximum of five horses when she was on the lorry because we always took out one partition so she had a double space. And it gave me great pleasure that in the last few years of her career she would arrive at an event having eaten her haynet. Result. One year she came back from Burghley weighing more than when she did when she set off from the yard to go there!

The weakness in Tilly's body had gone in the time since I first rode her, but her balance was very much still downhill, which isn't the nicest feeling as a rider. She certainly didn't blow me away, but we got to work. With the flatwork, I did a lot to get the right side of her temperament and to make her feel as loose and supple as possible, but once she learnt her movements she was, on the whole, pretty good when she was actually in a competition arena. I don't think there was one test where she made a big blunder. She stayed "with" me, listened and tried. That set her apart from other horses who might have been "better" than her. She gave her heart and body to me; she never got lazy in the arena or missed a change through lack of concentration.

It's all been about trying to get her to have more presence; "smile", believe, and be a bit of a showgirl. I love getting horses to feel like they are winners—that confidence in themselves makes so much difference. Although she wasn't impressing me, she was interesting me, and I wanted to try to improve her.

This picture from Belton in 2017 looks nicer than the round I had! She would sweat up a lot for each phase, and I still rode her in the bit that Paul Tapner had used on her, which was a gag with roundings on. At this stage I wasn't totally convinced by her, but I was enjoying training her

Our first run together at Oasby in March 2017, when I figured out she was quite nappy to the start box and would get herself hot getting to the cross-country—again, not ideal when I wanted to get a relaxed feel from her and to encourage her to gain weight

BACK IN THE START BOX

My first event in 2017 with Tilly was Oasby, and I realised she was going to be pretty hot. She's a funny little mare with plenty of intelligence and knows exactly what's going on; she went off to the dressage without a care in the world. When I got back on for the showjumping, she didn't particularly want to leave the lorry; she was hovering away from the cross-country and sweating up.

I think she'd got quite tricky to warm-up for both the jumping phases—before showjumping, I think there were times that they were lucky they were

At home and starting to build a partnership. Tilly's coat is coming through, there's no white sweat and she's starting to put on some condition. She was happier when travelling, and she was eating. Not sweating up the moment we started jumping was a bit of a turning-point, and we were starting to become friends

able to jump one practice fence. I like to warm up, of course—you want to feel as prepared as you can be—but she got really wound up in the collecting ring. In the actual ring it was the story of her life—she gave me no feel whatsoever and you'd hear her hit nearly every pole, but they didn't actually come down. That never changed!

I went down to the cross-country at Oasby and remember struggling to get her into the warm-up, let alone the start box, and at Oasby the warm-up is absolutely huge! Once we were through the start box and on our way round the

track at Oasby, she went sweetly—bravely, a bit snatchy in the contact and again, not a lot of feel over the obstacles, but I always believed she was going to jump every fence and that she knew where the flags were. She wasn't a strong horse who pulled at me and I was never going to lose control, but she could be unsettled. I wanted her to relax; ragging her round one-day events to pick up points was never going to help with settling her for the bigger days.

In time she learned to settle for the jumping warm-up and was pretty normal in the end, but the cross-country start was always something we had to manage throughout her career. It was pretty clear from the beginning that we needed a system to get her to the start box warmed up and ready to go but without getting wound up.

I would get my partner— and later husband— Thomas to put her number

These three pictures from the CCI4-S at Houghton in 2017 show the new relationship between us developing. I always showjumped her in a 'bubble bit' with the rein on the snaffle ring, and from then on she went cross-country in a rubber gag snaffle a soft mouthpiece and just a cavesson noseband. She was never a strong mare; it was more about balancing her than having to apply the brakes*

on the board and to call me when there were a couple of horses to go before us. I would just get on, trot into the warm-up area, canter, jump one fence and lob around until I was called to the start a few minutes later.

At the bigger three-day events when you have a set start time we worked out that if she was accompanied, she was fine. She didn't want to be led—she would pull back if there was any control, or physical pressure on her mouth in that situation—but my head girl Amy and my sister Nini would walk next to us, one either side of her head and Thomas would follow behind so we could almost herd her in the right direction. To be honest, the biggest problems were at the lower-level one-days and we never had a disaster at one of the big ones, but we were always very careful, knowing in the back of our minds that it was a possibility.

I did a couple more events that went in a similar way. I remember going to Belton for our first CCI4*-S together; we were getting by, but it still didn't look that calm or impressive. A very good friend came up to me and said, "Do you need to be riding a horse like that? Be careful about what you are doing."

To be fair to that friend, who is clearly a horsewoman, and to be fair to Tilly herself, I knew that I wasn't where I wanted to be with my training. I felt that every time I did something, a tiny bit more went my way. I could see a path, however much improving there was to do with both her mental and physical states, and I wanted to keep working with her.

Tilly always got very low over her fences and hit plenty of them, but she never did anything to frighten me. If she needed to do something quick with her legs and feet, she did it—she was never stupid, and she could be cat-like. And I always had Paul Tapner's voice in the back of my head, telling me she could jump the big stuff. That was something I kept trying to believe in. I think, when she was galloping and jumping jumps, she would have been happy with anyone on her back. She felt that was her job. But I needed her to let me in—to feel that we were in it together.

THE TURNING POINT - BRAMHAM 2017

After we'd ticked a few boxes in the early part of the 2017 season, I decided to take her to Bramham, the big event in Yorkshire. I had to do a CC4*-L (a three-day-event, as opposed to the one-day-events I had done with her up to then) to qualify for CCI5*.

I was fairly terrified walking the course— Bramham is big and, as I've said, she didn't get very high over her fences. I wondered if I would be able to balance her, especially if she got tired. She gallops with her head low, which is a pretty disconcerting feeling—I call it truffle-hunting, as though she is a pig snuffling along the ground searching for truffles.

But that cross-country day changed everything; it was a massive turning point in my feelings about Tilly. We set off, and she felt like a different horse. She was settling into a good rhythm and jumping out of her stride. Finally she must have felt able to relax and gallop, and the difference was extraordinary.

This is the fence before the water at Bramham, which she jumped well. But then she stumbled, and you can see what happened when you turn the page. I was so impressed that she stayed upright and kept jumping

Bond Dickinson

Having survived the dramatic moments in the water at Bramham in 2017, she jumped the next fence with her ears pricked and as though nothing untoward had happened! How brave, clever and honest of her

She was super-clever through the "coffin" (rail- ditch-rail) combination—and then we came to the water towards the end of the course. I am not quite sure what happened—did I get a completely wrong stride? She jumped into the water very well; whether she then had a slight stumble, I'm not sure. In front of us in the water were two big, fat brush boxes. I'm on absolutely nothing, thinking, 'Oh sugar—what do I do now?'

I just dropped the reins, kept my leg on and sat tight. It was over to Tilly now. We were on such a bad stride that I really couldn't do anything to help her—she had to decide what to do.

And she just kept going, scrambled over with her ears pricked, somehow kept herself—and me—upright—and galloped away after them, happy as larry.

Honestly, I cannot express enough how brave, clever and honest she was to jump those two narrow brush fences—most horses just wouldn't have done. Never for once minute did I feel I was going to be unseated—but the pictures look horrific!

It's amazing how much one round can instil trust and faith. From then on, I knew how to do it; I sit on the back of the saddle, practically on her tail, and I try to help her with her balance on a long rein. It helped that she went in just a soft rubber gag bit, didn't pull and that I could turn her on a finger-tip touch and that she was always looking for the next fence. If I had needed to have shorter reins to land and then make the turn to a second element of a combination, it might not ever have worked.

What a turning point that day at Bramham was. I was in awe of what Tilly had done. We finished sixth—a good result, but far more importantly I started truly to believe in her. She was a three-day event horse through and through.

OUR FIRST FIVE-STAR TOGETHER - BURGHLEY 2017

After Bramham, I started to get quite excited about taking Tilly to Burghley. We did the CCI4*-S at Hartpury in August as our prep event—which became our go-to routine every year—and still she didn't give me the feeling that she was a future Badminton or Burghley winner.

I'd been struggling with her on the flat, and she'd tied-up a couple of times. Thomas turned to me the week before Burghley and said, 'This is a pain in the arse. Is she worth it? Are you sure you want the aggro of all of this?!' He was speaking out of frustration and because he could see that I was finding her very stressful. There was a lot of hard work and management involved with Tilly, all the time, and it often felt like a pretty thankless task.

Off we went to Burghley, though. She tried her hardest in the dressage—she didn't let me down, and her score of 43.7 (that was before horse sport's governing

Burghley 2017: I felt that Tilly's lateral work needed to be more uphill and to have more presence; that kept improving with age and training, and she developed more self-carriage and a more advanced outline as the years went on

body, the FEI, changed the scoring system to remove the co-efficient, which thereafter made marks appear much lower) stood us in good enough stead.

It was my first five-star with her, and she could probably have won it. I hadn't ever really nailed Burghley before—I'd got round, but I hadn't ever made the time, so I didn't quite have the knowledge of how exactly to ride that famous, undulating track in the most efficient way.

Tilly puts fences behind her very quickly— she'd be half a second quicker away from them than any other horse, and that is a lot of time saved. And as much as she gallops with her head low, she was always in self-carriage and listening to me, and her feet were always underneath her.

We were clear across country with 3.2 time- faults, one of the quicker rounds

Tilly always looks 'smiley' in her extended trot pictures— it seems to be her party trick. Smiling gave her presence and belief, and those two things gave her the best marks. The Cottesmore Leap is one of Burghley's most iconic fences, and when you look at the cameramen in the ditch, you can see how massive it is!

of the day, and if I had known her better, we could have been faster.

It was all very exciting—we were in fifth position going into showjumping, and, remarkably, she left all the poles up and we finished second to Oliver Townend and Ballaghmor Class. I realised then that these really big events, which require real grit, toughness, character and endurance, were her days. I don't know why, but that is what she was made for and where she shines. Suddenly, this ordinary little mare had got within touching distance of a CCI5* win.

CHAPTER FOUR

FINDING THE KEY TO FUTURE SUCCESS

"Sometimes horses—even ones that perform at the very highest level—don't fit into a mould. You can only ride and train the horse you have"

AFTER THAT VERY eye-catching second place at Burghley in 2017, we were naturally on a bit of a high. But then I was asked to bring Tilly to some British Eventing team training sessions—and very quickly felt deflated. She's not "classically correct" and a lot of people don't understand her. Having her and her way of going, and how I rode her, analysed didn't do either of us any good. I've been part of British squads since my Young Rider days—it was all stuff I knew, but it didn't work for Tilly.

Twice in team training situations I got off her and cried—at my age! So I stopped taking her. I don't want to sound like I know it all or like I'm a spoilt brat, and of course I appreciate training and want to improve—of course I do. It made me feel so disheartened though, and was starting to do me harm. I am very self-critical anyway, and when you started to analyse her, there was so much "wrong". Sometimes horses—even ones that perform at the very highest level—don't fit into a mould. You can only ride and train the horse you have, not the one

This picture from the showjumping at Burghley in 2017 shows exactly how she did it—not giving them much height—but I had to learn to accept her unclassical way of doing things, to trust her and not to interfere with her too much

you—or someone else—wants that horse to be.

Ian Woodhead, who has helped me with my dressage since I was in my early 20s, and who is one of the most respected and popular trainers on the circuit, is the one who has really helped me crack it with Tilly. He didn't talk about what she can't do, and if he did, it was always in a positive way with a solution: "It might feel awful but it looks brilliant," he'd say. I've never had a single negative training session with him.

I worked out a plan that meant I wouldn't let Ian see me at a big three-day event with Tilly until 15 minutes before her test time. He'd say before that I was "fannying around", but I knew what I needed to do. I'd get her used to the venue and get her feeling supple and confident. I'd canter her about and maybe pop a jump. I knew what she would accept, mentally and physically, and I'd get her to the place where Ian could make sure we had a test outline and that she was responding properly to the aids, making her look as smart as possible. When she did a test, the difference when she "smiles"—when she has her ears pricked, her eyes are bright and she is ready to show off—is a whole mark, even though she would be moving in the same way in both situations.

I asked Ian for his thoughts on us, and he said: "Tilly wasn't built the right way to be a conventional dressage horse, so it was a case of working out how to manufacture her way of going so she looked like one.

"She was quite a cranky mare in the early days but in the last couple of years of her career, we knew how much we could push her and when we couldn't. At competitions you would hack out, letting her go with her nose on the floor. Then 15 minutes before her test I would say, 'It's time'...

"Tilly was very heavy in her shoulders. The compromise we came to was that she had to work in the outline, but we would never ask her to do it for more than 15-20 minutes. If you kept her there for longer she would throw her toys out and say, 'That's enough.'

Tilly at Oasby 2018. These pictures totally sum up the feeling Tilly gives me at a run-of-the-mill one-day event, and how I remembered her feeling as a young horse. There's not a great deal of effort being made! The difference between these and her at one of the major three-day events is so striking

Our rather spectacular nosedive into the water at Badminton in 2018. Our competition was over in a soaking split-second, and I really thought that the chancee of winning a five-star on Tilly was gone

"I know you didn't always know if it looked good or not, but you trusted me. Time and again you'd come out of the arena and say, 'What was it like, then? It felt horrendous.' I'd just say, 'Look at the scoreboard.' It was a two-man team at the big competitions. It needed the eyes on the ground."

Ian had great faith in Tilly, believing that one day she would win a five-star.

"She's relentless and has the biggest heart of any horse you'd ever meet. She did it all against the odds. She wasn't classical with any of it, but she was a galloper. You [Piggy] were brilliant with her—you're very good at getting to know a horse's brain, and would never push a horse over the top. You could never force Tilly to do anything and once you got her to an event you had to get her into the right frame of mind.

"I feel proud to have been a part of her career. Out of all the top horses I train, Tilly was the one that had the most going against her because of her conformation. That makes her one of the best. She was bred to do it, but not built to do it."

HIGHS AND LOWS

Tilly had two runs before Badminton in 2018— the Open Intermediate at Oasby, and then the CCI4*-S at Belton, where she went well and finished second to Jonty Evans and Cooley Rorke's Drift. So I was looking forward to having a go at Badminton—I felt we could give it our best shot, and that we had a real chance of achieving the time across country, or at least getting very near it.

I think it had been a wet spring and the ground was drying out by Badminton at the beginning of May, so it was definitely going to be a stamina test. That was the first year of the new scoring system, and she did her very best to manage a competitive mark of 25. We were 10th after dressage, less than five marks behind Oliver Townend and Ballaghmor Class, who led on 20.8—well in touch, anyway.

We set off across country and she felt amazing. I think I took the straight route through the Lake, which was causing lots of problems, and she was well on her minute-markers and skipping across the top of the ground.

It was funny—when I walked the cross-country course and came to the Hildon Water Pond on the far side of the Vicarage Ditch area, I thought to myself, 'Someone's going to do something stupid here.' There was a log pile and then a downward slope to a sort of hanging log with water trickling down it that you jumped into the water itself. It wasn't particularly big, but it just invited horses to "dive" at it a bit. I don't know why I thought that—it wasn't as if Tilly had ever done anything silly before—but water is the only thing that she does have a little look at.

I think she probably glanced at the water, held her breath slightly and, as ever, was a bit down- hill anyway, and we ended up doing a rather spectacular nosedive over the log into the water.

That, in a soaking split-second, was Badminton over for us.

To be honest, I can't see how I could have ridden it any differently. It was just one of those things. Tilly was completely fine afterwards— there wasn't a mark on her—but it was very frustrating. I knew that any rider and horse gets very few shots at a CCI5* victory, and here was one that was playing right to her strengths of grit, gallop and toughness, and it had gone.

Onwards and upwards. We didn't do a great deal in the summer except build up to Burghley, although Tilly did win the Advanced class at Aston-le-Walls which acted at the final trial for team selection for the World Equestrian Games in Tryon, USA. She was short-listed for the British team that year—the only time she was, I think—but the selectors chose another ride of mine at the time, Quarrycrest Echo and Tilly went back to Burghley instead.

We performed perfectly respectably at Burghley to finish fifth, but I couldn't help thinking that our chance of a five-star win had been washed away in that pond at Badminton.

Burghley 2022: Amy and Tilly at the prize-giving. Their relationship has been a key part of this story

TILLY'S PERSONAL SLAVE

My head groom Amy Phillips has been a vital part of Tilly's journey. Her care for her, her patience with her, and her love of her has been exceptional. Amy has a racing background, and she says she loves a tough mare who stretches her neck out and fights to win. I think that helped Amy develop a lot of respect for Tilly very quickly, which was great because she is, without doubt, a horse who needed a close relationship with, and a lot of understanding by, the person caring for her. In the final few weeks before a major event, we were walking a very fine line with Tilly in terms of her body and her mind, and Amy always used to laugh and said that she was Tilly's personal slave. Amy's whole day revolved around Tilly in the last three weeks before Badminton or Burghley.

I thought it would be interesting to hear about Tilly and her foibles from

Amy's side of things.

Amy remembers: "I started at Piggy's yard in 2018, so Tilly had already been second at Burghley by then—I had actually been working for Oliver Townend, who won that 2017 Burghley on Ballaghmor Class, beating Tilly, so I was aware of her.

"Tilly can be a bit of a witch in the stable if you don't know her; she'll make faces, and will lift a back leg at you if you ask her to move over. But in some ways she's very easy. She loves going out in the field and walks in and out like an old dobbin—we used to lead her with both Piggy's sister Nini's horse and Max's

pony, the three of them together. She's not very keen on other horses, but she likes those two.

"She comes in from the field into her stable in the morning, and she sleeps quite a lot and lies down flat with her head on the bank of shavings next to the wall, like a pillow. Then, when it gets to about 2pm, she starts chatting to you because she's bored, she's had enough and she wants to go out again.

"She's always the same when you tack her up. I guarantee she will poke her nose in the air when you want to put her bridle on, and that she will get hold of your clothes with her teeth and tug on them. She's not keen on a bath and has a little strop about it, and she hates being lunged— she finds it very boring. She's very good to clip; she hates you brushing under her belly, but she doesn't mind you clipping it, for some reason.

"Tilly's favourite event is Burghley. The autumn time suits her better than the spring, and she's always better in herself then. Burghley has a quieter atmosphere and the layout of the horse walk round the edge of the park, rather than straight through the middle, suits her temperament better than Badminton's does.

"My favourite phase at a big event with Tilly was the cross-country, because I knew I didn't have to worry about her—she'd be fine. She'd jump anything and would always look for the flags.

"As soon as an event is over, she knows it. After Burghley, which is only an hour away from us, she'd always come home and go straight out in the field that evening."

A FAMILY AFFAIR?

My sister Nini French has played a key part in Tilly's career. She did a lot of her fitness work and rode her whenever I was away at other events. Nini would take her for long rides where they'd be out for an hour and a half or so, getting fit and

My sister Nini French has been an integral part of Tilly's journey, and has always done the majority of her hacking and cantering at home and riding her whenever I've been away

keeping her life varied and interesting—I didn't do a lot in the school with her, and that worked very well.

Tilly is a very sensitive mare and you need to give her your full attention when riding because she could switch from being very lazy to being very hot and slightly mad just like that. You need to be able to feel that about to happen and use tact to prevent it. Tilly's always had very flat feet and thin soles, so riding her on ground that wasn't good enough, or letting her step on the smallest of stones, could cause a real problem. Hacking her took a lot of brain work to keep her in the right physical shape and the right frame of mind, and Nini always gave her 110%, never for a second skimped on anything or got distracted, and rode her beautifully. That is Nini all over with horses. If she does a job for you, she does it to the very best of her ability, and I would have struggled without her in so many ways over the past years. She was always there on cross-country days at the five-stars and worked very well with Amy Phillips on that front—they respect each other's knowledge and experience.

Nini says: "She goes through all the emotions on a hack. She'll start off like a slug, needing a Pony Club kick, then she can be bobbing along nicely, turns back into a slug, then turns into a nutter in the flick of a switch and suddenly boils over, turning white with sweat. Five minutes later, she's dry again and perfectly happy.

"I spent my life looking at the ground while on her, picking and choosing where to go. She's always been hacked on her own—she settles better and we just found it easier. All of the above meant I went on quite unconventional hacks with her; we'd just scamper about, but I'd also be working her correctly. I didn't do a huge amount on the gallop with her—when she first came back to the yard she got rather hysterical about it and would sweat up badly, but she did get much better. She'd still be keen, but she'd settle.

"I'd go down to a big grass field where I know the ground is very good, trot round it four times, canter round it four times, then go to the gallop. Depending on where we were in her fitness pro- gramme, she'd go up once "nicely", then do two sharper ones. Then back down the gallop, trot up the road and walk home up the long driveway. It's a good work-out but not boring for her, and kept her head and body happy. She likes to know her people, and she is confident in those around her and happy in her life. All good horses take up a lot of your day, but Tilly more than any other.

"I also used to long-rein her quite a bit; when horses are old, they don't want 'drilling', and long-reining was a good way to move her about without putting weight on her back.

"For such a funny mare, she was relatively simple to look after at the major events and not difficult to handle. She knows she is there to do a job, and she'd stand quietly at the back of her stable, happy in her own space. She'd be grazed in hand a lot, and by the end she was eating well when at an event.

"She definitely knew when it was cross-country day and would quiver when she was tacked up, but she'd walk calmly down with Amy and me on either side of her. And after she'd finished, she'd get given fluids without fail, but, extraordinary mare that she is, she never tied-up at an event—just beforehand.

"Although we learnt so much about how to manage her, she still nearly always tied-up in the last two weeks before a big three-day, whatever we did. You'd leave the barn thinking, 'When's she going to do it?' And she's so tough that she doesn't give you a huge amount of evidence that she has tied-up.

"Riding her on a daily basis, Tilly has never smacked you in the face as being an amazing horse. You know it is easier for some horses—they have naturally got a great jump or fantastic movement. She has to bust a gut to do her best, and she knows it. You have a very small window when she can perform at her absolute peak, but she tried so damn hard. That's what makes her special."

Burghley 2018: Tilly is improving more than I am in the dressage arena—she is becoming more uphill in her lateral work, whereas I could definitely be less crooked. I'm not that proud of how I look in this picture...

LAND ROVER
32

Left: I think 2018 was the first year that these great big white oxers appeared at the Maltings, and all riders were concerned about the size of them. See what I mean about Tilly being an out-and-out five-star horse? She's sailing over this, yet you can see on p49 that at a one-day event she doesn't look to have any scope at all. There was a third element to the Maltings complex; we're getting close to being at the buckle-end of the reins, but our eyes are firmly on where we've got to go next

Above: I love this unusual action shot. You can see how packed the crowds are at Burghley, which adds so much to the intensity of it all, but Tilly is thinking about me and isn't at all distracted by her surroundings

Right: Not Tilly's prettiest angle, but we're loving the cheer from the crowd at the Burghley prize-giving and she's shaking her head with excitement at another top five-star placing

CHAPTER FIVE

AT LAST!

"It was then that the world sort of exploded"

WE DID OUR usual couple of quiet runs in the early part of the 2019 season—Oasby and Belton—and turned our gaze on Badminton again. This year, however, I took Quarrycrest Echo ["Red"] to the American CCI5* at Kentucky—which was the week before Badminton. It was all quite a whirl- wind, Amy and I doing a major event with Red and leaving Tilly at home to do her final prep work with Nini, then flying back and basically going straight to Badminton. You kind of need everything to go right—there's no wriggle-room in that schedule.

Amy wasn't going to get back from the States with Red until Thursday, and would come straight to Badminton, where Nini would be with Tilly. And I also had our small son Max to factor in—I wouldn't have seen him for the week I had been away, and was about to turn round, repack and go to Badminton. Thomas—who normally is with me for every bit of the big events—would stay at home with Max and not come to Badminton until later in the week. My emotions were going in different directions anyway, and extra hassle wasn't going to help.

Tilly's dressage test at Badminton in 2019 was one of the best of her life for a score of 26

So when I rang Nini at the weekend, just a few days before Badminton started, and asked, 'How's Baggage?', meaning Tilly, I could have done without her telling me the mare had tied-up badly. She'd never done it that close to a competition before and I was terrified.

Nini says: "My life went on hold for 48 hours—she was on fluids, and I couldn't ride her until Tuesday of Badminton week. I gave her a tiny little ride on the Tuesday, and she felt ok, so we put her out in the field on Tuesday night. She looked fine at 5am on Wednesday morning, so I packed the lorry, trotted her up and off we drove to Badminton, going with the attitude that if she wasn't right, Piggy would withdraw her."

I'll say it again—Vanir Kamira is an extraordinary mare. She passed the first horse inspection without any dramas, as usual, and I gave her a good work-out on Wednesday evening at Badminton— which she had to have if I was going to get a decent test out of her, and to see if her body could stand up to it. She felt totally her normal self, so, without ever feeling comfortable about it, really, I decided to keep going, bit by bit, and if at any point she felt less than 100%, to pull her out. I knew I just had to keep in my Tilly bubble—she didn't ever feel mega, but that was her and I had to keep believing in her and in our system together.

She did her dressage test on the Thursday— the first day of dressage—and pulled off one of the best tests of her life for a score of 26—I definitely didn't want to go back and have another go; I was delighted with that!

It's weird. I watched quite a lot of other riders do their tests, and you think, 'Wow, look at that—they'll definitely beat me', but they made a couple of tiny mistakes, and we didn't. It's amazing how much difference that accuracy and reliability on Tilly's part makes. At the end of Friday I was fourth behind Oliver Townend's two rides and Tom McEwen with Toledo De Kerser, and I was over the moon to be in that position in a field like that.

She was pretty perfect across country, coming home two seconds over the time for 0.8 of a time- fault. You always kick yourself, thinking back to where you could have made up those two seconds, but she'd been so great, galloping along in her truffle-snuffling way, determined to get us over those massive fences and home safely. I couldn't have asked for more. We'd completely put the previous year's fall behind us, and we were second after cross-country with Oliver Townend and Ballaghmor Class 5.3 penalties ahead of us.

Tilly flew through the trot-up on Sunday morning, and then we waited for the clock to tick round to the final showjumping session in the afternoon. I know it looks like we could have won from our position—second, so without that last kilo of pressure of being in the lead, but Oliver had a rail in hand and a time-fault, and Tilly just never gave me that awe-inspiring feel that probably does make you think you're going to win.

She warmed up for the showjumping fairly well, in her fashion, and I went into the main arena with the usual feeling of having no idea whether she'd have every fence down—although she never has, it felt like it could happen—or jump clear. I wasn't much the wiser as she made her way over the fences: she did it by Braille, going tap-tap, with her ears pricked, getting lower as we neared the end of the track. I kicked on for the finish line as I was aware that the time was tight, and I think I was 100th of a second or something inside the time allowed. I'd felt her hit so many fences that I didn't know whether or not we had gone clear until I looked up at the score- board. By some twist of fate, we were absolutely clear, jumping and time.

It was then that the world sort of exploded. I remember leaning down on Tilly's neck and saying to her, 'I can't believe we just did that!' I was still a bit frozen with shock—I had been so focused on what we were trying to achieve, that it took me a moment to realise that we had done it. Then I looked up and saw and heard the clapping and cheering, and I stood up in my stirrups, punched the air

Here we are skipping over the huge logpile in front of Badminton House, and sailing over the Footbridge with ease. Compare these to the images of her practically falling over far smaller fences at her one-day events!

Her considerable speed and stamina meant that Tilly was always very close to getting the time across country at her five-star runs. She was just two seconds over the time at Badminton for 0.8 of a time-fault

and raced round the arena. It was just the best feeling, and I could genuinely feel the support from the crowd, so I did it again. And again. It wasn't about—at that stage—finishing second at Badminton, or any result at all. It was about my horse and me having done everything we possibly could at this legendary event, the pinnacle of my sport, and it was just the most brilliant feeling.

I came out of the arena not caring what happened. I was buzzing, and when I saw Thomas and Max, I slid off Tilly and just pulled them into my arms. It's a cliché saying that being a mother changes your perspective on life, but it does, so much. I'd been away from Max for what felt like so long, and I just wanted to

I couldn't believe that Tilly had showjumped clear for me, and felt so grateful and proud of her

Punching the air: I look distinctly more excited that Tilly does here, but I promise you that she was loving the attention of the overexcited Badminton crowd too! What a fantastic feeling it was finally to win a five-star

hug and hug him. I was in such a happy place—Tilly and I had done the most we could do, she had busted a gut for me, and I had my family there with me. I felt immense pride. I was content—whatever happened next.

Clare Balding had told me in the morning that she'd got her money on me winning, and I'd rather shied away from it, thinking it couldn't happen and I didn't dare dream that it would.

Oliver went in to jump. I heard he had knocked a fence down from the gasp of the crowd, and then I heard a few people saying, "He's going to be slow, he's going to get time- faults", but I wasn't really there in my head. I could tell that he had jumped the last—the crowd cheered, but it wasn't the sort of cheer you get when you've won, and the first light began to dawn in my head. I think, I think, I have won Badminton. Oh my God. In fact, Oliver had picked up 1.6 time-faults as

Finally holding that famous silver trophy, which was synonymous with Badminton for many years

well as his four faults for a fence down—and his 5.6 penalties meant I had won by 0.3 of a mark.

Clare Balding, who was just a few feet away, turned to me, and I knew. I hugged Max even harder—he's fortunate I didn't stop his circulation completely, poor kid—and all hell broke loose. Thomas had been watching at the barrier to the arena, and he legged it back towards me with this enormous grin on his face. He is such a stalwart support to me, and so good for my brain and my approach to this crazy sport, and I wanted to do it for him as much as anybody, to show that it was worthwhile, the ridiculous life we lead.

It's always a team effort, but Thomas is so important. You need someone who supports you, but doesn't blow smoke up your backside; who can get to the heart of it and tell it to you straight but whom you trust completely. He knows what winning Badminton meant to me, to us. My father's voice message sort of summed it up: "About bloody time, darling". I'd been second before, but if you want to be what we all set out to be when we're young and naive—the best at what we do—then you have to win the big ones. I grew up believing that Badminton and Burghley were the ultimate goals, and I still do. It is so very easy to have a "successful" career and not win either of them, and knowing that I had won Badminton was as much a relief as it was a pleasure, if you can grasp that.

For Trevor Dickens, it was everything. He had set out his stall that his mare was a five-star winner, and now she was. He always believed she could, and good on him. I hadn't shared that belief, but this scrappy, ordinary little mare had punched her way to victory at the most famous event in the world. I remember putting an arm around him in the prize-giving, saying, "Steph will be looking down on this now with such pride as well." These moments are family days as well for so many of us, and I know she would have loved to have been part of it all.

I've yet to ride at the Olympics, despite being agonisingly close more than once. I'd love to say I had done that, because the wider world under- stands what that means. But the horsey world appreciates Badminton is a far more demanding test of horse and rider than today's Olympic format. It is more difficult, you need to be braver and just better, really, and horse people get that. The words "Badminton winner" attached to your name put you in a tiny group right at the top of the sport, and define you, in a way. I wanted and needed that title, and now I had it, courtesy of Vanir Kamira.

THE AFTERMATH

As we eventually arrived home that night from Badminton, we were greeted by home-made signs of congratulation lining the lane to our drive, put up by friends and neighbours. There were more in the yard, and Tilly's stable was festooned with decorations. We had a bit of a spontaneous party, but once the adrenaline and the intense emotions drain away on an occasion like that, you are totally knackered.

Home-made signs lined the lane to our drive as we made our way home from Badminton

Tilly went to stud fairly soon after Badminton. During the six weeks she was there, she had four embryos taken from her, using the prizes given by Twemlows Stud Farm to the highest-placed mare at Burghley. As a result, she now has three offspring who were born in 2019—a chestnut mare by Chilli Morning (so both her parents are Badminton winners), one bay gelding by Jaguar Mail and one bay mare by Upsilon.

The amount of people who got in touch to say well done and how pleased they were that Tilly and I had won Badminton was overwhelming. I really felt a wave of support, which was lovely. Neither Thomas nor I are "party people", particularly, but Badminton felt like such a massive thing and I thought we ought to acknowledge it in some way, and celebrate it properly.

There was another thing, too. Thomas and I had been engaged to be married for three years by then. Every time the subject of a wedding arose, we'd talk about it for five minutes and then move on to something else. We had no idea of how we wanted to do it, or when, and there was never enough time or money, really, so we just put off thinking about it yet again.

Not long after Badminton, Thomas and I were driving back in the car from competing at Chatsworth, and I said, "I think we should have a Badminton party for close friends, the people around us and the people who are either very current in our lives right now or have been with me on the journey of becoming an event rider somehow. And, once everyone has arrived, we should turn it into a surprise wedding."

I wanted to get married from home,

Thomas and I on our wedding day, with three-year old Max

in the very cute church in the village, with our son Max there. But the church only takes 100 people, and once you start making a "normal" wedding list, it very quickly gets huge— family you haven't seen for years and years, everyone who has ever asked you to their wedding, and so on. You seem to be at 250 people before you've blinked, which would have been impossible.

I found it all too much to contemplate, particularly with the eventing season in full flow. I also didn't want people to worry about what they were going to wear, or to buy us a present or any of that sort of thing. So we thought—if anyone is enough of a friend or supporter just to come to a party to celebrate Badminton, then those are the people we'd like at our wedding.

We made a phone call to a good friend who had helped me as a PA for years, Sara Fowler. I knew how professional and discreet she is, and that anything she organised would be very classy. Bless her, in less than six weeks she did the most superb job of pulling together the party/wedding that we wanted, and I will never be able to thank her enough.

I am totally clueless about this sort of thing, but I did know that I needed a wedding dress. While I was competing at Houghton Hall in Norfolk, which is very near to where my Mum lives, she produced a couple of dresses that she had ordered online that she said she thought might suit me. You can imagine—I'd been eventing all day, so I was sweaty, dirty and stressed. Ideal for trying on wedding dresses. But, amazingly, one of them was just right—thank you very much Mum, that will do, job done!

It was a total secret, which was rather cool as there was no hype and no stress (except for poor Sara). It was close enough to Badminton that everyone was still delighted for me and there was a buzz about it. It was just something to look forward to, rather than worry about. Afterwards there were a few people who hadn't been able to come who said they would have somehow made it if they'd known it was our wedding, but that was rather the point—come if you can, come

This was taken at the same time that Horse & Hound came to do a feature about Tilly a few days after Badminton. What a strong, happy, healthy girl—she looks great. You can also see how flat her feet are, and that her soles are very close to the ground, which has always been one of the difficult parts of her we've had to manage carefully

and celebrate with us, but no worries if you can't.

We had a lovely day. It worked perfectly in every way. Badminton was the best day of my career, if not my life, and this just topped it off. We were surrounded by great friends, the people we love, and we were very happy. If Tilly and I hadn't won Badminton, I doubt Thomas and I would have got round to getting married yet, so that's another thing that little mare did for me!

CHAPTER SIX

NO FOOT, NO HORSE

"My Badminton heroine refused at the fence into the water complex—and only just crawled in at the second time of asking. Not ideal"

BADMINTON AND BURGHLEY were now the usual book-ends of Tilly's seasons. Reading that sentence back to myself emphasises once more how extraordinary she has been, how game, how brave and how tough, that the two most demanding, competitive events in the world were always part of her calendar.

However, our progress towards Burghley 2019 was bumpy. I never really enjoyed riding her at one-day events; she didn't see a lot of point in them and was always less than inspiring in the feel she gave me at them. She was a three-day- event horse, through and through—she needed the big occasion and the galloping, strong cross-country course to shine.

I took her for a little pop round the Open Intermediate at Keysoe, though, the week before Burghley—just for an outing and to canter round on very good ground.

But my Badminton heroine refused at the fence into the water complex—and only just crawled in at the second time of asking. Not ideal. There was another

Tilly jumping—reluctantly—into the water at Keysoe in 2019, having refused at it. We then discovered that a change of farrier had caused her to have hoof problems, and were able to rectify the issue by using pads

water jump later on in the course which, like the first one, had a decent- sized drop to it, and she didn't feel great over that, either. Tilly is a horse who genuinely feels like she'd jump through fire for you, so I was really worried.

When I took her off the lorry and walked her out to her field that night, it was apparent to me that she was feeling her feet a bit. We always trot them up when they get home after an event, but it was actually when I was walking next to her, rather than when I saw her trot, that I noticed it—she was just a little shuffly. She's always had bad, flat feet and they are quite delicate, and she's had the same farrier, Stephen Green, for the entire time I'd ridden her. He's done a wonderful job with her, but she'd been away for a while, at stud and so on, and just a couple of shoeings by someone different had had an adverse effect.

I rang Stephen immediately and he put some special pads on Tilly to act in a cushioning way and to help reduce the concussion. She felt much better, and I schooled her through our water jump at home, which is very horse-friendly, not too deep and has excellent footing to it. She didn't bat an eyelid now her sensitive feet were no longer sore.

Most unusually, she didn't tie-up that year before Burghley—clearly she'd given us enough worry at Keysoe to keep us on our toes!

BURGHLEY 2019

We went to Burghley 2019 as CCI5* winners; part of an absolutely tiny group of horses and riders to have conquered one the sport's highest peaks. Tilly and I had achieved what I had dreamed of since I was a little girl, building fences from sticks in the garden and jumping them again and again on my feet and pretending I was my heroine, Mary King.

I'd been second at Badminton on Jakata in 2011; you get that close to the top of the podium and you wonder whether you'll ever get the chance to climb on to the top step. Eventing is so hard—so many things have to come together at exactly

Making the long walk down to the cross-country start at Burghley in 2019 with my sister Nini beside us. Amy Phillips and her wheelbarrow are not far away, as ever

A cool shot of me looking at the scoreboard at Burghley in 2019. A rather nice set of marks!

Tilly jumping through Defender Valley at Burghley in 2019 with ease and looking very confident. I had actually forgotten my body protector. I'd just come back from the European Championships and it wasn't until I was getting ready for cross-country that I realised I'd left my normal one at home and only had my Team GB one with me, hence looking a bit different in this picture.

the same moment, and I can tell you that there's far more heartbreak than ecstasy. And if you are lucky enough to find the right horse, with the ability, the brain and the will to do it, and you are good enough to ride and train it, that horse has still got to stay sound.

You manage them as carefully and as well as you possibly can, but the demands of the training, the fitness work and the actual competing are considerable and the smallest thing can throw everything off balance. Keeping Tilly right and producing her to that twice-yearly peak was to tread a very fine

Brave and brilliant as Tilly is, jumping an upright gate on her wouldn't be among my favourite things to do! The top picture shows the infamous white gates at Burghley in 2019, which caused quite a few problems, and on the right we are jumping (climbing?) over a gate at Burnham Market in the CCI4-S*

line—a tightrope, really. But, although her feet were a weakness, she had four excellent limbs and was basically a very sound horse, which helped enormously.

Her owner Trevor says he knew she would win a five-star. In my heart of hearts, I don't think I ever believed she could—but do you ever? I don't know. Perhaps with a more obviously talented horse who gives a rider that mega-star feel—but then, will that prodigy have the heart and the guts?

And, having done it once, it's a completely different ball game doing it again. How many horses win two five-stars? Especially if those two are Badminton and Burghley?

As ever, she gave it her best shot at Burghley. I was delighted with her dressage mark of 26.9. Once again she gave me a "clear round" of a test with no mistakes. I knew I had milked the crowd and the applause at Badminton, and I did wonder whether she'd light up a bit in front of a crowd this time, but she was level-headed and listened to me.

We did something very cool that year, and were "double clear" across country—no time- faults as well as no jumping penalties. Tilly was two seconds under the time, and the only horse to stay on her dressage score at the end of cross-country. Burghley's track is always very serious, but that one in particular caused problems. I really didn't love the double of white gates course-designer Mark Phillips had placed at the bottom of Winner's Avenue—Tilly never felt like she got particularly high in the air over anything and often bellied her way through brush, as you can see, and I was very glad to get those gates behind us.

For the first time she felt quite tired between the three- and four-minute markers on the track, so I sat a bit easier on her and gave her a kick at the top of the downhill bits, let her fill her lungs up, and she tigered her way up the hills. She was such a little fighter. Her head would go down, her ears back, she'd grit her teeth and say, come on Mum!

After cross-country, Tilly and I ended up 0.1 of a penalty behind my great friend Pippa Funnell and MGH Grafton Street. Pippa has tons of "proper" showjumping experience, of course, but both our horses had scrapped their way round an enormous cross-country track the day before, and we knew anything could happen.

In the end, we both had a showjump down. Tilly hit the first fence—she probably rattled most of them, but that was the only one that fell—and then Pippa ploughed through the planks. We stayed first and second, and although you always want to win, I couldn't have been more thrilled for Pippa. It was 16 years since she had last won Burghley—2003, the year she took the Rolex Grand Slam—and 14 years since she'd triumphed at a five-star. Her horsemanship, her patience, persistence and kindness is such an example to all of us in the sport and anyone who rides a horse, and she deserved another top-level success so much.

AND THEN CAME LOCKDOWN

Good old horses are like good old lorries—their diesel engines tick along nicely when they're in their routine and being used regularly. The moment you stop with them is when the problems start. Tilly's schedule had worked very well for her for the past few years—with the odd heart-stopping moment for me, along the way—and when the world came to a grinding halt in March 2020 when the Covid pandemic took hold, it was hard to know what to do.

We had no idea how long we would be on lockdown for, and what sort of sport we would eventually be able to resume. She wasn't a horse I did very much with in the school, and for quite a long time we couldn't even do any meaningful hacking, which is what she had thrived on with Nini for so long.

I am fully aware of how lucky I was, to be at home with my husband Thomas, our son Max and our key staff, with so much space around us and horses to ride. Plenty of younger horses benefited from the pause, and the chance to take a breath and consolidate training. Tilly's generation of out-and-out CCI5* horses lost out, though, as it was only at those big events that they could excel.

Badminton 2020 was cancelled and Burghley followed. We had managed two Open Intermediate runs before lockdown, and I did pop her round another one at Cholmondeley at the beginning of August. There was no three-day event for Tilly to target, however; Burnham Market hosted a CCI4*-L and the eight- and nine-year-old CCI4*-S usually held at Blenheim that autumn, and riders and owners were very grateful to Alec Lochore and his team for doing so. But a smallish, tight track was never going to be our mare's cup of tea and it wasn't worth wasting a run. We'd just have to hope that 2021 would see some return to normality.

2021

In the end, 2021 was a hotch-potch year. Tilly went very well at the spring Burnham Market fixture to finish second in the CCI4*-S on her dressage score and we were full of excitement about Badminton. Then the plug was pulled on it fairly late, to our disappointment. Again, Burghley followed suit.

Helen West and Andrew Fell stepped up at Bicton, and off we trundled to Devon for first a CCI4*-L in June and then, as a one-off, pop-up Burghley replacement in September, a CCI5*.

At the June CCI4*-L Tilly performed her usual consistent dressage test and bombed round the cross-country - one of only a handful to make the time - and was in second after that phase. However, the flatter showjumping cups and maybe jumping on an artificial surface, rather than grass, left us with four poles rolled on the final day to drop us well out of contention. To me she didn't feel she jumped any differently to normal, but I guess the way she rubbed the lighter poles on those flatter cups didn't work out for us. The reality of four fences down was one of those things that I always knew could happen - luckily, that was the only occasion.

A few months later, we went back down south for the five-star. It wasn't

Burghley—you couldn't replicate that majestic site with tens of thousands of spectators—but they did a brilliant job in what were crazily uncertain times.

I didn't really have any idea of how Tilly would go, after two years of doing virtually nothing, and it seemed a long time since she'd given me the "five-star feel" that I only got from her at the most serious events. But she got it—this was a big one—and she grew into her five-star persona.

We were second after dressage on 25.5, a mark or so behind Pippa Funnell and Billy Walk On, and she absolutely ate up the cross-country. The fences weren't perhaps the hardest ever seen at a five-star, but Bicton is properly hilly and the terrain made it into a proper test on what was a hot day. I said to *Horse & Hound*

Good to get going again at Burnham Market in 2021. Tilly looks like such an ordinary little mare here - who would have thought she'd won Badminton and been second at Burghley?! Showjumping at the Bicton CCI5 in 2021. Tilly lost her lead with two down, but still finished third. This is what I mean when I talk about Tilly truffle-snuffling— galloping along with her head on the floor, which was a feeling I took a while to get used to!*

that, "she puts her snout down on the floor and off she goes." I always felt like I was sitting right at the back of the saddle with my feet forward, but that was how it worked so well. I steered and stayed in balance; she looked for the flags and galloped her guts out. There were four narrow brush fences in a line towards the end of the course, and I wondered when we'd skimmed our way through them whether there was any brush left in them, but she always seemed to know just how high she needed to get—and not an inch more.

Pippa had a few time-faults and Tilly was seven seconds under the time, so we jumped up to the lead. The showjumping was never going to be a walk in the

Here's Tilly in her winter woollies being run up in-hand by Thomas in December 2021. It was taken at our Christmas owners' party, where we do drinks, a barbecue and mince pies, and then bring out a selection of horses for people to see. It's always funny to see how normal these smart event horses look when seen out of the eventing season!

park, though. Bicton has an impressive grass main arena and they use very flat cups. As much as I wanted it for her, another five-star win didn't seem particularly likely.

In the end she had two down—I actually thought, when we crossed the finish line, that it had only been one—and dropped to third. Gemma Tattersall won her first five-star, on Chilli Knight, which she thoroughly deserved. In the press conference afterwards Gemma's boyfriend Gary Stevens asked her to marry him, which topped off a pretty fab weekend. Both Pippa Funnell and I enjoyed attending their wedding the following year.

The Bicton CCI5 podium - Gemma Tattersall on top, with Pippa Funnell and I either side of her, having a right old go with the champagne*

Delighted to go into the lead in the dressage at Bicton. And very big pats for Tilly!
Max looks pretty happy about the whole thing too—he's caught on to the excitement here

CHAPTER SEVEN
A ROLLER COASTER SPRING

"I should have been so excited to be back at Badminton for the first time since Tilly and I won there in 2019, but I felt totally depressed"

TILLY CAME THROUGH the winter of 2021/2022 looking really well, and Badminton was the plan once again. We went to Burnham Market in April as usual to do the CCI4*-S, and that turned out to be an awful day. Thomas's sister Caroline was competing in the CCI3*-S and had a very bad fall. She was knocked unconscious and had spinal injuries, so there was a long delay before she could be airlifted off to hospital.

It was very tough—there's your sister-in-law, who's had a terrible accident, but there's also your job to do on owners' horses. As a sports person you have to be able to put yourself in different places mentally as required. After a conversation with the March family, who told me that there was nothing that I could do to help at that moment and that I should get on and finish competing, I withdrew all the horses that weren't due to go to Badminton and went cross-country on Brookfield Inocent and Tilly.

I ran and got on Tilly and went straight in to showjump, and I don't think

The scoreboard froze during my dressage test at Badminton in 2022, so no one had any clue what my score would be. I am looking over to ask people, 'Was that any good?' With Tilly it is hard to tell whether we've done a really good test or not as she doesn't really ever give you that magic feel—but her accuracy and the effort she puts in has meant some very good scores over the years

I knew whether I was coming or going. Horses are such weird, intuitive creatures—perhaps somehow she knew that I wasn't OK and that I needed her, and she jumped what was probably one of the best rounds of her life. What a friend she was to me. She was great across country, too, but what had happened that day was to set the tone for the next few weeks.

Caroline was in hospital, and it gradually became clear that her spinal injuries meant that she was going to be in a wheelchair. We all know that there are risks involved in riding horses, and that accidents can occur anywhere, at any time, but it's only when it happens to a person you are really close to that it becomes real.

There was already a black cloud hanging over us, therefore, before Badminton. Brookfield Inocent was injured after Burnham Market; obviously that was nothing compared to what had happened to Caroline, but it was another brick in the wall, as it were.

Eventing is a very close-knit community, and by the time I'd been at Badminton for half a day, every single person I saw had asked me about Caroline, about whom the news wasn't positive, and also to say that they were sorry about

Delays caused by falls before we started the cross-country at Badminton in 2022 meant that Tilly didn't really switched on during the early part of the course. As soon as we turned for home, however, she found an extra gear completely and set off like a racing car, coming home one second over the time

Brookfield Inocent. I'd spent hours and hours discussing all the bad things that can happen in the sport, and I admit I went back to my lorry and had a good cry. I then fell fast asleep—I think my brain was just totally fried, and I found it hard to think of a single positive about being at Badminton. I should have been so excited to be back there for the first time since Tilly and I won in 2019, but I felt totally depressed.

Tilly's very glossy and rounded bottom!

However, as I said, the brutal truth is that you have to be able to compartmentalise things in your mind in sport. I had to pack into boxes Caroline's situation, the fact that I was leaving Max and Thomas at home when I desperately felt I wanted to be with them, that the horse on whom I'd won team gold and individual silver on at the 2021 European Championships was broken, and get on with the job I was there to do.

My dressage was on Thursday and, good girl Tilly, she put her best foot forward to score 25.7. That put us in equal sixth, with Laura Collett and London 52 first on an incredible mark of 21 and Tom McEwen second with Toledo De Kerser on 23.4. Both Laura and Tom had been part of the British team that won gold at the Tokyo Olympics in 2021, along with Oliver Townend. Brookfield Inocent and I had originally been asked to go out there as first reserve, but I thought flying all that way and not competing would have been completely the wrong thing for the horse, so we stayed at home and went to the Europeans instead. Another Olympics missed, but that's probably all a story for another

Big pats again after the Badminton showjumping phase in 2022. It had been three years since she won there, and to finish fourth at the age of 17 after so much disruption in past seasons was very impressive

day— this is Tilly's book.

My warm-up plan with Tilly on cross-country day is very important. I don't do masses of work with her, because the longer you are out there with the noise and buzz of the cross-country going on, the hotter she gets and she'll start to get quite nappy, even after all these years.

We executed our normal routine—I get on half an hour before my time, it takes 10 minutes to walk to the practice area where I go straight into canter, then jump a few fences—but just enough to warm up her muscles and get her thinking in cross-country mode. Then we check her girth, I have some water, or a sweet, or put on some lip balm—all three are always in Amy's bag, and I choose which one; it's just part of our ritual—and then it's time to walk up to the start box in the main arena, with Amy and Nini on either side of Tilly.

I heard on the tannoy that Tommy McEwen and Toledo had fallen. That was upsetting as they are a great combination, and I'd had them down as the winners that year. It was clear that the course was causing real trouble—barely anyone had got home at that stage. The horse in front of me was in the start box, at which point you know you've got four minutes to go until it's your turn, and someone came up to me to say that the course was being held because Nicola Wilson had had a fall.

Your instant reaction is that your all-important routine has been interrupted, which is not good with any horse and especially not with Tilly, but immediately your question is, "Is she ok?" and your worry about your great friend takes over. Nicola and I had had a quick hug and said, "Good luck, bird, kick on" to each other just an hour before in the lorry park—she's always been one of the nicest people in eventing, and we'd won team gold together at those Europeans in Switzerland the previous September, where she'd done so brilliantly to win individually and become European Champion.

The answer to my question was no, and that the screens had been put up around her, which usually indicates something serious.

I took Tilly back to the lower warm-up area, which is quieter, and got off her. Nini led her round and she went from being very alert and up for it to quite switched off again. The course was held for about 45 minutes, I think, which is a long time for the emotions to escape their boxes and rush through your head. My sister-in-law was in hospital, probably paralysed, my lovely friend now was on the ground with the screens round her. I was walking about fairly aimlessly, keeping myself to myself, and I saw this man sitting on an old trailer on the edge of the field on his own. I kept looking over, thinking, "I know him", and eventually realised that it was Nicola's father. What do you say to someone in that situation? He looked at me and said, "Why do you girls do this?"

We all now know that that fall ended Nicola's riding career. Luckily, and unlike Caroline, she is not paralysed, and with her remarkable, endless positivity and amazing attitude, Nicola is once again part of our sport—training, commentating, judging, and smiling her way through everything as she always has done.

Back at Badminton, I got the warning that the course would be restarted in 10 minutes. You have to get back on, refocus and streamline your thoughts to you, the horse and the course in front of you. Tilly had gone very quiet and sleepy; she was quite happy, but she definitely wasn't fired up. I jumped the showjumping practice fence a couple of times and she felt fine, but once we set off, it took me two to three minutes to feel as though I could really get her into gear.

She left a leg quite badly at Huntsman's Close— luckily it was a brush, so she could stay on her feet and keep on her line, but it didn't feel good. Even by the first minute-marker she was behind on time, and I was nudging and pressing her to go without getting a lot of reaction. I was surprised that I didn't have the engine beneath me that I normally had, and it went through my mind that she might have tied-up; the interrupted warm-up, my weight being on and then off and then on her again, the increase and decrease in adrenalin due to the disruption. I thought that if I got to the third minute-marker and she hadn't picked up, I might just pull her up by Badminton House, which is where the entrance to the stables is, and accept that today just wasn't her day.

But she started to feel better, if not quite her normal vrooming self—I remember working harder than I had done before at the Vicarage Vee and fences like that, and I had to kick and say, "Come on, old girl". She's a funny old fish, though—she jumped the solar panels fence, where Tom McEwen had fallen, and when she landed she took over like a racing car. It's as if she knew that from that point onwards, we were homeward bound. She set off and it felt like I needed my seatbelt! She must have made up 30 seconds in time from there, which is unbelievable. She just put her head down—truffle snuffling again, although at supersonic speed—and said, "Hang on Mum, we're going."

She came home only one—annoying—second over the time, and I was thrilled with her. It had felt like she had had to dig deeper than ever before, though, and when she just tipped one showjump the following day, aged 17, with all that had happened since her victory in 2019, I was very proud of her. I knew I wasn't going to win—Laura Collett and London 52 were out in front, and Tilly and I ended up fourth—but I still had a good old punch of the air. I was filled with so much pride, and respect for Tilly. What a brilliant result, and what a strange, clever animal with a huge heart she is.

CHAPTER EIGHT

BAGGING THE OTHER 'BIG B'

"The moment we got to Burghley, you could just see in Tilly's face that she was happy to be there"

THE SUMMER OF 2022 was a dry, hot one. The ground was hard, which never suited Tilly's flat little feet, and I just began to think that she was starting to feel like an older horse. In such a contrast to her earlier years, she'd started to get quite fat, and was a broader, stockier girl than the racing snake she'd once been.

I thought a couple of outings where she'd stable away from home would trim her up a bit, so she had one Open Intermediate run on good ground at Burgham in Northumberland, and then she went to the CCI4*-S at Hartpury for her usual pre-Burghley outing.

Hartpury was a very competitive field—all the World Championship prospects were there, and what do you know, she won it. She'd become very consistent, and the nicest thing was that she was mellowing in her mind. She was obviously happy to be there—she did a lovely dressage test and showjumped clear, which put her into the lead before the final cross-country phase. She was 17; realistically I knew our days were numbered, so I thought we'd try to have a go. I kicked on and she whizzed round to finish on her dressage score and beat all those very smart horses years younger than her.

Dressage at Burghley in 2022 and Tilly scoring a personal best mark of 22.6. I was so proud of her, and I love that you can see her improved self-carriage and core strength

Tilly found the cross-country at Burghley in 2022 harder work than she had done before, but she tried her best and dug deep, as ever, and went into the lead on Saturday night before the final day

Maybe the onlooker would have thought she was exactly the same as she'd always been, but I thought she was operating at just a bit below her best. She was a little jarred up afterwards—remember how brown and burnt the grass looked in late summer that year—and we wrapped her up in cotton wool, hoping we could get her feeling 100% for Burghley.

I was at another event two weeks before Burghley when I got the call from Nini to say that Tilly had tied-up again. Not badly, and probably because the weather had changed and it had finally started to rain, but it was enough to make me really question whether we were going to the well once too often with her.

Tilly was my head girl Amy's whole life for those last two weeks—she barely left her side.

I drove to Burghley thinking, "Should we be going? Should I turn round and

Tilly jumping her way to the most incredible Burghley victory at the grand old age of 17. She looks amazingly well and shiny here, which is such great credit to my team at home

say, 'Enough'?" But the moment we got there, you could just see in Tilly's face that she was happy to be there. There was something about her mannerisms, just the way she was, that she absolutely loved being at Burghley. She was so settled and comfortable there. For all her great achievements, Tilly has never stopped being a snakey, sharp little thing—Amy will tell you—but she was lovely that week; just incredibly pleasant to be around and she just seemed to have a big smile on her face for the whole event.

You do develop a serious bond with these horses over such a long period of time. You share so much with them; you have to trust each other and know that you can rely on each other, and you have these little moments together, when you're on the hack up from the stables to the main arena or something, where you feel like your minds are in tune and you can communicate with them. I said

I felt such a wave of appreciation from my friends in the sport as we came out of the main arena having won, and it meant a lot to have Thomas's arm around me and Amy and Nini on our other side

to her, "Come on, girl— one last push now together. We can do it."

I didn't think her dressage test, as good and as accurate as it was, was necessarily any better than her other recent efforts, but the judges awarded her the best mark of her career—22.6. I was hoping for a PB—personal best—because she had really established her core strength and more self-carriage at the ripe old age of 17 and again, she just didn't make mistakes.

Tilly flung herself around the cross-country in her usual gritty, tough way. There were a lot of big, wide fences and I felt she was right at the top of her scope jumping them and I was having to nudge her along at times to keep her up to time. But the trust between us meant that I hardly even touched the reins, let along took a pull, on the run home from the Cottesmore Leap at the top of the track. Ears flat back, she galloped through the finish one second over the time (again!) and she still took some pulling up afterwards.

I knew she'd given her all for me, and, miraculously, we went into the lead.

LAND ROVER
ABOVE & BEYOND
1-9

Anticlockwise from above: Grinning my head off with the Land Rover trophy and Burghley House in the background. Thank you, Amy—we couldn't have done any of it without you. Queen Bean in apples and carrots to welcome Tilly home! Trevor Dickens and I cutting the Burghley winner's cake. Tilly's own Burghley-winning cake, with her mates Amy and Nini, before we left the Burghley lorry park to drive home to Maidwell

Only the other awesomely tough mare, 19-year-old Classic Moet, ridden by Jonelle Price, was faster than Tilly and made the time. Neither mare would inspire to look at, or to ride at home, but somehow they were made for five-star eventing.

Tilly trotted up well on the Sunday morning, but I was pretty apprehensive about the show- jumping. I had a fence in hand, but you can never take anything for granted, and although it had very rarely happened, her habit of rattling her way around a showjumping track meant that it was slightly in the lap of the gods as to whether the fences stayed up or not.

I'm very much a believer that you prepare as best you can, you take your training to the event and you do your best—that's all you can do. But I was desperate for it to be Tilly's day. I wanted her to go out on top; in my mind she was a Badminton horse and a Burghley horse. She'd won one of those, I really, really wanted her to win the other, because she deserved to.

I hadn't been able to sleep at all the night before; I was wriggling about and going over and over everything in my mind, so before the showjumping on Sunday I took myself off and did my Christmas shopping to distract myself.

Anyway, off we went. She hit the second and third fences, and I thought, "Crikey, we could easily have three fences down here". In fact we used up our "life" quite early on in the course, but I made myself stay focused and I could hear that there weren't too many gasps and groans from the crowd. I've said this a million times, but Tilly's a funny horse—you can't help her too much, because if you do, she loses the shape of her jump. You have to trust her front end, which is really hard when you're slithering over fences, but if you start to support too much or try to hold her front end up, she doesn't finish her jump off behind and will have it down with her back legs. It's about riding her balance and staying as much in the middle of her as possible, but not supporting too much with the rein. Not easy when every instinct tells you to "help" her.

I remember glancing over at the scoreboard after the second-last and thinking, if I can just jump this and not do anything stupid, then she's going to be a Burghley winner. She cleared the last, landed, and of course I set off like a mad thing, galloping round and round the ring like a lunatic. Round and round I went, and you know what, it was bloody brilliant. Tilly loved it—she was grinning like a Cheshire cat, too, and zooming round the arena to absolute roars from the crowd. They knew how special she was and what she'd achieved in winning Burghley and Badminton.

In some ways, it was a relief. Badminton had been hugely thrilling because it was unexpected—I hadn't been in the lead, Oliver had—but here all the pressure was on me and Tilly. Once that pressure burst, I was just flooded with relief, delight and so much emotion. There were so many smiling faces as we came back into the collecting ring—the respect of your peers means so much—and I couldn't wait to grab Thomas and Max. I'd grown up in Norfolk so Burghley was my local "big event"; I'd ridden there in the Pony Club showjumping competition, and it had been my first five-star, two decades earlier on my Young Rider horse, Flintlock. Winning it was desperately important to me, and it was so fitting that it had happened on Tilly, who had turned from a very ordinary novice horse I hadn't much wanted to ride into the ultimate five-star competitor.

Amy says that when she turned Tilly out in her usual field at home that night, she went over to Nini's horse, Harold, and roared at him like she was a stallion—she was so pleased with herself, the clever old bird!

I was so happy for Trevor Dickens, whose belief in his mare had been unwavering, and I was so happy for myself and my family and team, whose support had been so crucial. But most of all I was happy for Tilly, who had proved that heart, guts and will to win were more important than anything else.

One last blast round the CCI4-S at Burnham Market in 2023, finishing second and beating many of the horses destined for Badminton that spring. She went very well but I knew I wanted to leave it at that*

Tilly's three four-year-olds, who were born by embryo transfer, seen at Trevor Dickens' home in July 2023. From left to right: Bramble, Bella and Billy. I look forward to seeing more of them in years to come

CHAPTER NINE

BOWING OUT

"It was so important to me that she finished having 'done enough', not having 'had enough'"

NOW WE GET to the last chapter, and it was time to make the decision about when to retire Tilly. This was actually quite a difficult decision, but probably more for her owner Trevor than for me.

She came out of Burghley very sound and well, but hadn't enjoyed the year that we had had on very firm ground after an abnormally dry summer. It felt harder work for her. This was definitely a stage that I never wanted to get to with her. I wanted to finish her at the top of her game, sound and loving it rather than waiting for her form to drop off — or, even worse, being lame. I thought we would be greedy to continue and I would never have forgiven myself if anything had happened to her or she didn't enjoy her life anymore. I owed her more than that.

She came out at the beginning of the 2023 season as an 18-year-old and looked an absolute picture. She didn't look like an old horse at all, but she did feel older to work. She went through the motions, but the training just was feeling a bit harder

PIGGY MARCH
GREAT BRITAIN
VANIR KAMIRA
2022

work. She did, however, pop around one Open Intermediate at Lincoln in sweet style and then stormed round Burnham Market CCI4*-S to be only one of two inside the time and finished second in a very hotly contested field.

She did feel as low as she does like to go, though, and I did kick her round the whole way saying, 'Run, Tilly Bean, run!' She has always loved that, but that last bit of bite wasn't there. I gave her a big pat coming through the finish, and in my heart of hearts I thought, 'This is it, my darling, this is it'. She pricked her ears and pulled up comfortably.

She had been to the well for me so many times and always gave me the feeling that she would have died for me. It had to be my call as it was just probably never going to happen without disappointment. It was so important to me that she

Commentator Spencer Sturmey interviewing me during Tilly's retirement ceremony in the main arena at Burghley in 2023. I was surprised at how emotional I felt!

Vanir Kamira and I enjoy one last blast round the Burghley arena, a year to the day after our victory there. The crowd gave us a loud, heartfelt standing ovation and it was a lovely celebration of her career

finished having 'done enough' not having 'had enough' and this was the perfect time. And thank goodness we did stop there. Badminton that year was so wet and a real slog for all the horses, conditions that she would have relished in her earlier days but at 18 I would have hated having to put her through it. Even Burghley that autumn for some reason caused some freak lamenesses, so in my heart I felt I had 100% done right for her.

Trevor found it harder than me to accept this decision as her form had been so great but I hope now, deep down, he knows that we were doing the best thing for her. I was very grateful to him at the moment he agreed to let her retire from competition. I felt fulfilled.

I kept her in work that season as I thought it was a shame and wrong just to stop work altogether. She loves her hacks, and lives in the field the rest of the time unless the weather is too bad. She basically does whatever she wants! She would still bite me on a regular basis and look like a velociraptor often over her stable door if anyone got too close to it, but she quite quickly switched off. She was always quite a hot and cold little mare but once she realised she was no longer a competitor she was quite the kick-along to ride! She is a very intelligent animal and was suddenly quite different. I was soon teaching my nieces on her in the school and riding out with Max on fun 'boy rides'. She loves it and I don't have to despair trying to keep her straight in left canter anymore...

We did do a little retirement ceremony for her at Burghley this autumn (2023), a year after she won there, which was lovely. She looked amazingly well and I had so many comments on how she good she looked. That meant a lot.

I didn't want to take the saddle off in the main arena that Sunday, as is often traditional in retirement ceremonies, as I felt that was too sad. I wanted to celebrate her career, and let her trot and canter round the ring once more, for which she received a loud, heartfelt standing ovation from a very appreciative crowd. I did feel emotional, but really just so proud of her. I know I will never have another horse in my lifetime with her heart, toughness and ability to deliver on those big days.

She walked back to the lorry that day as cool as a cucumber, ears pricked and taking in all the Burghley crowd and support. In her competition days she would have been jig-jogging and in a muck sweat, but as I have said before, she is an incredibly intelligent horse and somehow she knew life had changed. I had a lovely moment alone with her walking back to the lorry park that day. She was very content and just took it all in. It was quite funny, passing all those enormous Burghley cross-country jumps on our way back and remembering all our great rounds there and what she had done for me.

What a legend she is. I just gave her a big pat on a lovely long rein and said 'Good girl, Tilly Bean, good girl'. I will treasure our memories forever.

Amy Phillips and Tilly at Burghley in 2023. Tilly was relaxed and cool all day; she's a very intelligent mare and she knew that life was different now and that her competition days were over

ACKNOWLEDGEMENTS AND THANKS

I WOULD LIKE to thank Trevor Dickens for his persistence in trying to get me to take Tilly on. He asked me a lot, and I think at the sixth time I gave in!

Izzy Taylor and Paul Tapner for their bravery and skill in producing Tilly up to top level when she gave me a feeling I didn't believe in, or necessarily like, as a young horse. They proved me wrong, and I admire them a lot for this.

My sister Nini French, who rode Tilly whenever I couldn't, to keep her body and brain in the best place possible. This was invaluable to the horse, and to settling me when I was away a lot leading up to the big competitions.

Amy Phillips, who did so much for this mare. Their relationship was very special, and Amy's care towards Tilly was second to none.

Ian Woodhead for all his help and the belief he instilled in me and Tilly on the big days. She wasn't easy and he always saw the best in her. Ian believed in us, and I owe him a lot for that.

Catherine Austen for her time, skill and patience with putting my words to paper for this book. It wouldn't have been possible without you. And to Hilary Manners for helping pull it together.

My family, for their ongoing support of me, and to my long-suffering husband, Thomas, for keeping the wheels turning in my head when the pressure is on!

And to Tilly, of course, for making my dreams come true.

ABOVE & BEYOND

PHOTOGRAPHIC CREDITS

Huge thanks to the following for the fabulous collection of images charting Tilly's career:

1st Class Images, Hannah Cole, Benoit Herinckx, Trevor Holt, Libby Law, Nico Morgan, Peter Nixon, Thomas March and the team at home.